WHITE FLOWER DAY

By Steven Weissman FANTAGRAPHICS BOOKS, inc.

Editorial Coordinator: Gary Groth **Book Design:** Steven Weissman **Production:** Joe Preston and Paul Baresh **Promotion:** Eric Reynolds **Publishers:** Gary Groth and Kim Thompson **Dedicated to:** Charissa Chu **Thanks:** Mats!?

 Fantagraphics Books, 7563 Lake City Way NE, Seattle WA 98115. Call our toll-free number for a free full-color catalogue of comics 'n' related pop culture. 1.800.657.1100. Or visit us on-line at fantagraphics.com.

ISBN 1.56097.514.8
PRINTED IN KOREA

"I SAW YOU" (5), WHITE FLOWER DAY (57), LOOK OUT FOR BIG DELLA (78).

"I SAW YOU"
M. LIQUOR
W RIVERFRONT
MILLTOWN MUNICIPAL
JUNE 17, 2000

LLTOWN MUNICIPAL

TRANSFER, PLEASE...
CH-
CH'NG

JUST-SO

THANKS

JUST-SO

TRANSFER, PLEASE

YOU NEVER SAW ME
ZZT-

YES... MASTER

THAT'S A NEAT TRICK!
I JUST THOUGHT OF IT!

ADVAN
THE
ADVANCE

MOVE IT ALONG, BUDDY!

PLENTY OF ROOM IN BACK...
ADVANCED THEORY

LA LA

SO, WHAT DO YOU THINK OF LI'L BLOODY'S NEW POWER?
UH... PULLAPART BOY..?
I'M FEELING RATHER PROUD

HEY, MAN!!
RR!

YOU GUYS SEE THAT KID?
WHAT KID?
SHUSH!

THAT KID, A FEW ROWS UP... YOU CAN'T SEE HIM FROM HERE, HE'S TOO SHORT...
KORPSE

OH, LITTLE GUY? READING A BOOK?
THAT'S HIM
THAT'S WHO?
I CAN'T
THAT'S MY COUSIN!!
?

YOU HAVE A COUSIN?
OF COURSE I HAVE A COUSIN!
SAY

WELL, I'D LIKE TO MEET HIM!

GET BACK HERE, YOU!

AREN'T YOU GOING TO INTRODUCE US?
YAH
NO!
WHY NOT?

BECAUSE I HATE HIM!
OHH

THEN HOW'S ABOUT I GO OVER AND GIVE HIM A "LI'L BLOODY?"
SIT DOWN!
!

I DON'T EVEN WANT HIM TO KNOW THAT WE KNOW HE'S HERE!

BUT... HOW DO YOU EVEN KNOW THAT HE KNOWS WE'RE HERE?

OH, HE KNOWS WE'RE HERE, ALL RIGHT!
HUP.

WHEN WE GOT ON THE TRAIN? OUT OF THE CORNER OF MY EYE, I SAW MY COUSIN DUCKING DOWN IN HIS SEAT! PF... HE MUST'VE SEEN US COMING..!

MOST HORRIBLE!!
HE LOOKS NERVOUS

HE OUGHT TO BE NERVOUS! GIVING ME THE "HIGH HAT"...

...AND NOT TWO WEEKS AGO I WENT OUT OF MY WAY TO HANG OUT WITH HIM!

YOU DID!?
BUT
I THOUGHT YOU HATED HIM!
OH, I DO! BELIEVE ME, I DO...
YAH
SEE
...

ANYWAY, I WAS AT MY GRANDMOTHER'S BIRTHDAY PARTY...

LIKE HE'D EVER LET ME FORGET **COLLEGE BOY**! A YEAR AND ONE-HALF YOUNGER THAN I AND ALREADY A SOPHOMORE AT THE UNIVERSITY...

...THE NEXT COUPLE OF DAYS WERE WORSE THAN USUAL. ALL DAD TALKED ABOUT WAS MY COUSIN...

DID YOU KNOW THAT HE WON THE WILLIAM S. GRANT? MAYBE YOU SHOULD TRY SPENDING MORE TIME WITH YOUR COUSIN (INSTEAD OF THAT CROWD YOU CURRENTLY RUN WITH)...

...YOU NEVER KNOW!

...YEH, SO ANYWAY...

Z
LET'S GO, ELLIS!!
LOOK ALIVE!
315
JOY BAR

GOTTA KEEP 'EM ON HIS TOES...
...YOU WERE SAYING?
DONC

OH, YEAH... SO, LIKE... THAT VERY EVENING...

...PULLAPART BOY?
OH, THERE YOU ARE...
YES, SIR

THERE'S A TELEPHONE CALL FOR YOU...
?
DEEP!

I DIDN'T HEAR THE PHONE RING
PAW

HELLO?
PULLAPART BOY?
JA?
THIS IS COLLEGE BOY...

OH? OH, HEY... HOW ARE YOU?
IT'S OK
UH

DO YOU THINK YOU MIGHT LIKE TO COME BY THE UNIVERSITY SOMETIME?

I... I GUESS SO..!
I COULD SHOW YOU AROUND THE LAB... INTRODUCE YOU TO SOME OF THE GUYS

WELL, THAT SOUNDS FINE... WHEN?
IS TOMORROW GOOD?
OH, PROBABLY

COME AROUND NOON, THEN. WE'LL GET LUNCH
O.K.,
BYE
D'NK.

...BESIDES, JUST BECAUSE I DON'T HAVE A SCHMANCY SCHOLARSHIP DOESN'T MEAN I CAN'T BE A SCIENTIST TOO... YOU KNOW...

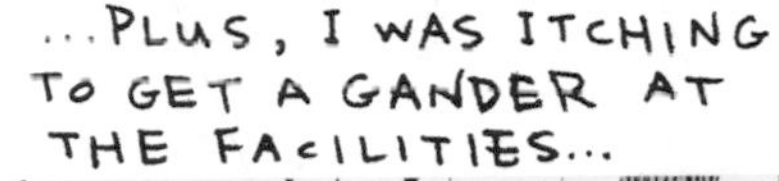

WELL
THANKS FOR COMING!
HOP

I'LL SHOW YOU AROUND ...UM... THIS IS THE LABORATORY...
UH-HUH

...AND THESE ARE MY LAB-MATES...
OH?

DAVID BEE...
HEE HEE

LEE LAND...
HI

...AND "CRUSH" IRVING
IS THIS THE COUSIN?
YES

HOW FASCINATING!
INDEED...
HM

AND YOUR UNCLE, HE REALLY DID ASSEMBLE THE BOY FROM YOUNG CADAVERS?
POKE!
TUG...
GOOD TEXTURE
PINCH!

YES, HE DID... WOULD YOU FELLOWS LIKE TO JOIN US FOR LUNCH?
OF COURSE!

YEAH..?
...AND?

SO, HOW WAS IT THAT YOUR UNCLE WAS ABLE TO KEEP THE DIFFERENT BODY PARTS FROM REJECTING ONE ANOTHER

WELL, HE INITIALLY NARROWED HIS SEARCH BY SELECTING MALES IN A SPECIFIC AGE AND ETHNIC RANGE...

OF COURSE, THE BOYS ALL HAD TO BE AMONG THE NEWLY DEAD...
NATCH

FROM THERE, HE CROSS-CHECKED BLOOD TYPES AND SO FORTH... STILL, THOUGH, MANY OF HIS PIECES HAVE YET TO HEAL AS A COHESIVE UNIT...
NAB!

...SEE? IF YOU LOOK CLOSELY... **THERE**... THE STITCHES WERE MEANT TO BE A TEMPORARY SOLUTION... BUT...

HOW ABOUT THE BRAIN? WHAT WAS THE SELECTION PROCESS LIKE FOR THE BRAIN?

HM... I'M NOT SURE... PULLAPART BOY? CAN YOU HELP US?..

HE, UH... I DON'T KNOW...

HUM...WELL... A PRIZE SPECIMEN, NO DOUBT... ANY IDEA OF HOW MUCH DAMAGE SUSTAINED WHILE IN TRANSIT?

UM... I DON'T SEE WHY THERE WOULD NECESSARILY HAVE TO BE ...ANY DAMAGE...

DON'T BE OBTUSE, COLLEGE BOY, SUCH A PROCEDURE WOULD TAKE HOURS!! HOW COULD THERE NOT BE SIGNIFIGANT BRAIN DAMAGE?!
POINT

JAB

CHU-CHU

OF COURSE, I WASN'T THERE AT THE TIME...

DO I EVEN NEED MENTION THE RECENT DEVELOPMENTS IN GENETICS AND CLONING THAT RENDER THIS LAD 100% OBSOLETE??

HAVE YOU NOT READ YOUR FRANKENSTEIN?
IT'S MONSTROUS!
GOOD DAY

HEH..
SO..

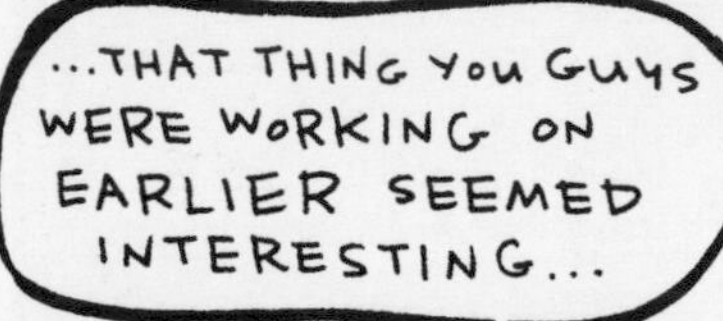
...THAT THING YOU GUYS WERE WORKING ON EARLIER SEEMED INTERESTING...

UH... UNDER THE MICROSCOPE.?.
?
WHAT'S HE.
YOU KNOW... THE—
OHH!

WELL...WELL, THAT'S KIND OF COMPLICATED, PULLAPART BOY...
ERM..
ITCH

OH, I DON'T MIND
OH!

PULLAPART BOY, ARE YOU FAMILIAR WITH MODERN FLYOGENIC THEORY?

OH, SURE... I USED TO EXPERIMENT ON FLIES QUITE A BIT...

UMN...
?
WHAA..

I THINK YOU MEAN FLYONICS, MAYBE, PULLAPART BOY..?
OH..?

WHY ARE YOU TELLING ME ALL THIS??
WE ALREADY HATE HIM, YOU KNOW!
JOING

BECAUSE, AFTER ALL THAT, MY COUSIN GIVES ME THE BRUSH?? ME!?
PF
SO WHAT
BOING

YOU SHOULD BE WITH US!! WE'RE YOUR FRIENDS, YOU KNOW!
THAT'S RIGHT!
BOING!

WELL, I JUST THOUGHT WE WERE GONNA DO FUN STUFF, LIKE EXPERIMENT AND JUNK..!
THAT'S STUPID!
I KNOW!

...BUT ALL THEY DO IS SIT AROUND AND TALK!!
STUPID!

FLANG!

HUFF!
HUFF!

CHUCK!!

SNATCH

WHAT'S THE FUSS?

THAT'S HIS FAMILY YOU'RE FRETTING ABOUT, AND FAMILY IS A PRECIOUS GIFT,, NOT TO BE TAKEN FOR GRANTED...

OH, YEAH? WELL, MAYBE YOU SHOULD STOP TAKING YOUR PRECIOUS GIFT FOR GRANTED AND GET THAT AVERAGE BACK OVER .300!!
YOU KIDS...
...YOU'LL SEE...
TROT

CHEE

C'MON, YOU TWO...

...LET'S SEE IF WE CAN USE LI'L BLOODY'S NEW POWER TO GET INTO THE BALLPARK FOR A CHANGE!
CAPITAL IDEA!
WHA?

AH, YOU'VE RETURNED
YES

YOUR COUSIN PHONED

...HE'D LIKE FOR YOU TO CALL HIM BACK AT HIS LAB...

OH, HE WOULD NOT

WHAT DO YOU MEAN "HE WOULD NOT?"
I MEAN:

I DO NOT BELIEVE YOU! MY COUSIN DID NOT CALL ME - MY COUSIN HATES ME!!

HATES YOU?!? DON'T BE RIDICULOUS!!
I'M NOT BEING RIDICULOUS! HE HATES ME AND I HATE HIM BACK!!

THAT'S A HORRID THING TO SAY!! YOU LOVE COLLEGE BOY!
YOU LOVE HIM!!
CLUTCH

OF COURSE I LOVE HIM, HE'S MY NEPHEW!
NO NO NO

YOU LOVE HIM MORE THAN ME!!

OH, FOR HEAVEN'S SAKE, PULLAPART BOY, THAT JUST ISN'T SO!
HA
HA

NO FATHER COULD BE AS PROUD AS I AM OF YOU TWO BOYS...
HUG!

...BUT IF YOU DON'T RETURN YOUR COUSIN'S PHONE CALL, I'LL GIVE YOU SUCH A WRATH!!

NOW BE QUICK AND PLEASANT ABOUT IT!
THH!
CLOMP

GET AWAY FROM ME!
FF

HH!

HELLO, COLLEGE BOY?
OH, HEY!
THIS IS YOUR COUSIN

YEAH, I KNOW...
DID YOU CALL ME?
UH-HUH

I TOLD YOU SO!
WHAT DO YOU WANT?

ER... I WAS WONDERING IF YOU WANTED TO HELP WITH AN EXPERIMENT I WAS CONDUCTING...
YOU WHAT?

YOU KNOW.. HERE AT THE UNIVERSITY? WE COULD WORK ON IT TOGETHER...
YOU'RE SERIOUS
YEH

BUT, WHY ME? WHAT'S WRONG WITH YOUR LAB-MATES?
...TO BE HONEST..?
I DON'T TRUST THEM

?
WHAT!
You DON'T KNOW WHAT IT'S LIKE HERE, PULLAPART BOY. THE PRESSURE, IT'S INTENSE! ...EVERYBODY STEALS YOUR IDEAS..!
HOT STUFF

WELL, I'LL BE DIPPED..!
IT'S TERRIBLE! BUT I KNOW THAT I MAY TRUST YOU...

You CAN? WHY'S THAT!
IT'S BECAUSE YOU'RE FAMILY

OH... OH, YEAH
DO YOU THINK YOU COULD COME TOMORROW?
BLUSH
TOMORROW?

BUT, THAT'S SUNDAY!
YEH, NOBODY WILL BE IN THE LAB THEN...
THE BUMS!

WELL... O.K., I'M SURE IT'LL BE FINE WITH DAD...
I'LL SEE YOU AT NINE!
SUPER!
CLICK

...NINE?
BZZZZ

PULLAPART BOY, YOU'RE LATE!

AM I?
YE-ESS...
WE AGREED ON NINE

YEH, BUT IT'S ONLY ... I MEAN, MY TRAIN JUST..?
LET'S NOT MAKE A BIG THING OUT OF IT, OKEY?
C'MON!

UH...
OK
EEK!

HEY, THERE!
HEY
BOY-GENIUS!!
A LITTLE HELP!
HA HA
C'MON

OH, BOTHER...!
?

UNGH!
BUNT

HERE, I'LL GET IT
Aww
HAW!!
HAW
OH, MY!

BOOTS!
AWRITE!!
WOO-WOO!

ALL RIGHT, COLLEGE BOY!! YOU FOUND A FRIEND WHO CAN KICK!
VERY CLEVER
LET'S GO!
HAK

COME ALONG, PULLAPART BOY...

DO YOU SEE WHAT IT'S LIKE FOR ME HERE?
DO YOU SEE?

IT'S AS IF THEY'VE NEVER SEEN A FIVE YEAR OLD IN COLLEGE BEFORE..!
UH-HUH
YAWN

THE ENTIRE STUDENT BODY KNOWS WHO I AM... I'M TIRED OF BEING ON DISPLAY
SWIPE

THEY SHOULD BE ON DISPLAY.. THEY'RE NEANDERTHALS!
BZZZZZ
TALLS
CH'K

SHORTLY, THOUGH, VERY SHORTLY, THINGS ARE GOING TO CHANGE AROUND HERE...
HOW DO YOU FIGURE?

IT'S WHY YOU'VE COME! IT'S MY GREAT EXPERIMENT!!
THAT!
OH, YEAH ...THAT

WHAT'S SO GREAT ABOUT IT, ANYWAY?
SO, YOU'RE CURIOUS? GOOD!

LOOK AT THEM, SO CONFIDENT IN THEIR ATHLETICISM...

OF COURSE THEY PICK ON ME, I'M FAR TOO CONSPICUOUS A TARGET!

AND SO, IN SECRET, I HAVE DEVELOPED MY OWN FORMULA FOR INVISIBILITY!
HERE

INVISIBILITY?
YES

FOR THAT HAS BEEN MY DREAM: TO WALK THIS CAMPUS-NAY! THIS CITY-UNMOLESTED AND UNRECOGNIZED!
HUM?

SEE, EVER SINCE I WON THIS SCHOLARSHIP AND GOT MY PICTURE IN THE PAPERS, THE PUBLIC SCRUTINY HAS BECOME UNBEARABLE!

"PUBLIC SCRUTINY?"
ONLY EVERYWHERE I GO!!

DOWNTOWN, IN THE MARKET OR AT THE GYM! IT'S ALWAYS THE SAME... CINEMAS... LIBRARIES...
MM-HM...

ON TRAINS?

ESPECIALLY ON TRAINS! LET ME TELL YOU: I WALK WITH MY HEAD DOWN, EYES TO THE FLOOR...

HOW AWFUL IT MUST BE FOR YOU...

WELL, I... I KNEW YOU'D UNDERSTAND.!.
UM...

...AND WITH YOUR HELP, PULLAPART BOY, I NEEDN'T FEAR MY OWN SUCCESS ANYMORE!
YA DON'T SAY
HEH

LOOK HERE, DARLING COUSIN! ALL OF THE ELEMENTS NECESSARY FOR THE CREATION OF MY INVISIBILITY SERUM!

AND **HERE!** LOOK **HERE** UPON MY FORMULAE!! YOU'RE THE FIRST TO SEE THEM! ARE THEY NOT **BEAUTIFUL?**

I-I CAN SEE THAT YOU'RE NOT IMPRESSED! ...WELL... IF YOU COULD BUT UNDERSTAND THESE FIGURES... **YOU WOULD BE!..**
SN'F

I ASSURE YOU, IF MY LAB MATES SAW THESE, THEY'D **FLIP!..** AS FOR YOU...WELL... **YOU SHALL SEE...**
SHUFFLE

...OR **NOT SEE!**
HE
HEE
HA
SMAK
UGH

O.K.! I THINK YOU CAN MANAGE THIS...
REALLY

...I'VE LINED UP THE INGREDIENTS IN THEIR MIXING ORDER, AND HERE ARE THE AMOUNTS TO ADD FOR EACH...

NOW, YOU'LL HAVE TO WORK QUICKLY, YOUR MEASUREMENTS MUST BE PRECISE AND DON'T FORGET TO STIR CONTINUOUSLY!
WAG
WAG WAG

I'LL BE RIGHT HERE, SYNTHESIZING THE KEY COMPONENT... SHOULD YOU HAVE ANY QUESTIONS: ASK.
LET'S DO IT!
YOU SURE LIKE TO TALK!

FFF...!

!

UH... COLLEGE BOY..?

EXCUSE ME?
...OH, BROTHER

HELLO?
EEEE!

HIMMEL!!

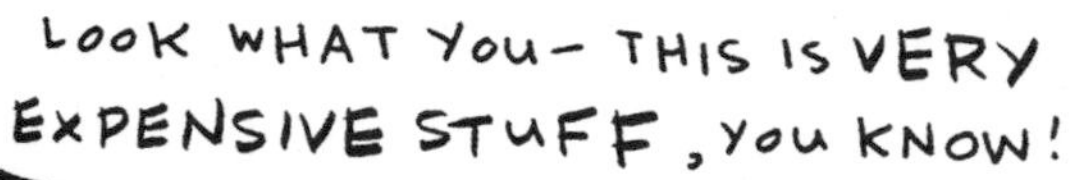
LOOK WHAT YOU– THIS IS VERY EXPENSIVE STUFF, YOU KNOW!

NOW I'LL HAVE TO GO DOWNSTAIRS FOR MORE OF IT!... MAN, THEY'RE GONNA NOTICE FOR SURE!
BUT YOU SAID TO ASK
HOP

DON'T TELL ME YOU CAN'T HANDLE THIS!

I CAN HANDLE IT

THAT'S GREAT!!

JUST STICK TO MY FORMULA!
YEH YEH

AND STIR CONTINUOUSLY!!
!

??

BEURK!!
SMACK!

HE CAN'T FOOL ME!..
FeZH

SCOOP

DUMP

THIS IS ALL JUST SOME LAME ATTEMPT AT GETTING ME TO THINK HE'S NOT A JERK!
SOME HOPE!
POUR

...INVISIBLE!..
FEH!

SHAKE!
SHAKE

...AND DOES HE GO ON? WAH!!
PAP

?

HO-HUM
SPOON
SPOON

"OH! I'M SO TIRED OF BEING ON DISPLAAYY"

"QUICK, EVERYBODY! LOOK!! IT'S THE BABY GENIUS..!"

"AW, JEE..."

"LET'S GIT HIS AUTYGRAPH!"
DRIB

POUF!

WELL, HOW DO YOU LIKE THAT?
WHICH REMINDS ME...
I'M HUNGRY

HUNGRY ALREADY?
WE'LL BE FINISHED SOON ENOUGH...
LUCKILY, I FOUND AN EXTRA SUPPLY DOWNSTAIRS...

HAVE YOU BEEN STIRRING CONTINUOUSLY?
YES, I'VE BEEN STIRRING CONTINUOUSLY...
CHEE

FABULOUS! KEEP UP THE GOOD WORK!
I-HOP!

BECAUSE... I'M NEARLY...

OH, C'MON

LA-LA!!

NOW, IF YOU'LL ONLY HOLD'ER STEADY...
I'M SO HAPPY...

DRAB

TOSS

MAY I?
I INSIST!

OOO, IT'S WARM!
I'VE BEEN STIRRING IT

NO, NO... THIS IS CHEMICAL WARMTH...
OK..
YAWN.

GL'G.. GL'G
WHA?
DON'T!

MMM... DISGUSTING!
I CAN'T BELIEVE YOU JUST DRANK THAT!

WHY? DID YOU THINK I WAS KIDDING?
YES!

WELL, I WAS NOT

HM...

I CAN SEE MYSELF...

SAY, PULLAPART BOY! CAN YOU SEE ME?
?
OF COURSE I CAN SEE YOU!

HUH, IT SHOULDN'T TAKE THIS LONG...
SAY!
WHERE'D YOU GO?
!
ARE YOU NUTS?

I'M STANDING RIGHT HERE!
?
INVISIBLE!!
TINK!!

THIS-THIS MAKES NO SENSE!.. UNLESS...

...UNLESS YOU ALSO DRANK THE SERUM!!
POUNCE!
STAY BACK!

ADMIT IT!
I DID NO SUCH THING!
I'M NOT CRAZY, YOU KNOW!
AM I REALLY INVISIBLE?

HOW CAN IT BE?
I DON'T FEEL INVISIBLE...
WHY CAN I NOT SEE YOU, THEN?
?

COME TO THE WINDOW!!
AWP!!

WHAT DO YOU SEE?
WHAT SHOULD I SEE?

UH, UH... ARE THOSE IDIOTS STILL PLAYING BALL ON THE GRASS?

YES, OF COURSE!
HA
HA

YOU MEAN YOU REALLY CAN'T SEE THEM? C'MON...
DISASTER!!

COLLEGE BOY, YOU'VE GONE BLIND!
NO!..
I HAVEN'T

I CAN SEE EVERYTHING!
JUST NOT...

...ANYBODY!!
?

THIS IS MOST HORRIBLE!..
BUT, HOW?
HOW?
!

OH, YEH? SOME REAL SCIENTIST YOU TURNED OUT TO BE! YOU WERE GONNA BE THE INVISIBLE MAN BUT NOW YOU'RE JUST THE VISIBLE KID!!
HAW

THAT'S RIGHT! MAYBE YOU DON'T KNOW SO MUCH... MAYBE YOU'RE NO BETTER AT SCIENCE THAN I AM!
YEAH

YOU?!? WHAT A SCREAM!!
PLOUPE

IF YOU'LL RECALL: IT WAS I WHO WON THE WILLIAM S. GRANT AT THE AGE OF THREE...
PAT

YOU'RE A WALKING ASSORTMENT OF KIDS TOO STUPID TO LIVE!!
TOSS

AND WHAT ABOUT THAT BRAIN OF YOURS, ANYHOW?
BONK!

LEE WAS RIGHT, YOU KNOW! THERE HAD TO BE SIGNIFIGANT DAMAGE THERE..!
BLECH..

OH, YOU'RE QUIET NOW, AIN'TCHA?
PF!
TAKE MY TIP...

WELL, I'M GOING TO FIGURE OUT HOW YOU DID THIS TO ME, YOU PULLAPART BOY!! NO SWEAT!!

...AND WHEN I DO, I'M GOING TO CORRECT YOUR MISTAKES AND COMPLETE MY EXPERIMENT!!

I'LL BE INVISIBLE YET, YOU HEAR?!

AW, NUTS!

JULY 11, 2000

BUT, YEAH... FOREST FIRES ARE A REAL DANGER, ESPECIALLY IN AUGUST...
HUM

WELL, I DON'T ENVY YOU GUYS... I MEAN, AREN'T YOU AFRAID OF ALL THE BEARS?
H'RF

BEARS!

I'M SERIOUS, FELLOWS! I HAVE THIS UNREASONING FEAR OF BEARS!!
HAH
WAUGH
ARF

THE WAY I HEAR IT IS THEY'RE MORE AFRAID OF US THAN WE ARE OF THEM!
MM...

PLUS, IF YOU EVER DO GET ATTACKED, ALL'S YOU HAVE TO DO IS LAY DOWN AND PLAY DEAD
YUP

SURE, A SIMPLE ENOUGH TRICK FOR THE TWO OF YOU...
OH,
HO
HO!

SAY... HEAR THAT?
BESIDES, IF IT WERE A
QUIET, YOU!
...YEAH, I HEAR IT, TOO!
...IT SOUNDS LIKE...

LET'S AWAY!!

!
THAT'S YOUR HOUSE!

I HAVE TO TALK TO YOU!!
OH, NO

THAT'S MY COUSIN!!

YOUR COUSIN FROM THE TRAIN?
THE VISIBLE KID??
UH-HUH
WOW

I KNOW YOU'RE IN THERE!
...HE'S RAVING

YEAH, HE TALKS A LOT...
OK, BUT SH!!
LET'S GET CLOSER!

HEY..
C'MON..!
WHY HAVEN'T YOU RETURNED MY CALLS?
I DIDN'T MEAN ANY OF THAT STUFF, YOU KNOW
I THOUGHT WE WERE FRIENDS!
THINGS HAVEN'T BEEN SO GOOD...
I HAD TO TELL MY WHOLE LAB WHAT WE'VE BEEN UP TO...
SO, WE GOT TO WORKING ON MY VISIBILITY PROBLEM...
THEY KNEW SOMETHING WAS UP...
I KEPT BUMPING INTO EVERYONE!

...AND TRIED EVERYTHING WE COULD THINK OF, I SWEAR

...WHATEVER IT WAS YOU DID THERE... WE COULDN'T REPLICATE IT...
SEE WHAT I MEAN?
CHEE!

WELL, THEN THE LAB SET TO WORK ON MY ORIGINAL EXPERIMENT
...

...NEED I TELL YOU THAT DIDN'T WORK EITHER?
TEE HEE!
BLA-BLAH BLAH-LA
HA

SHUSH!! I WANNA HEAR THIS!
!
!

YOU MUST RETURN WITH ME TO THE UNIVERSITY!!

I DON'T KNOW HOW USEFUL IT IS, BUT YOU'VE DEFINITELY HIT ON SOMETHING...
THEY SAY...

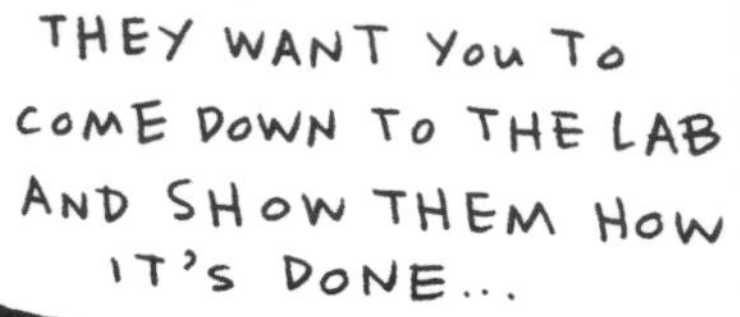

DO YOU WANT ME TO SAY THAT YOU'RE A BETTER SCIENTIST THAN I AM? THAT'S FINE!! DO YOU THINK THAT I CARE? I DO NOT

OK?

BUT REMEMBER: AS SUCH YOU HAVE A RESPONSIBILITY TO THE SCIENTIFIC COMMUNITY!

SO COME TO THE UNIVERSITY - SHARE WITH US YOUR KNOWLEDGE!

HEY!! WATCH IT!
UGH!!

EXCUSE ME!! I DIDN'T SEE YOU!
WELL!
I NEVER

OH
OWTCH
HEE HEH...

WHAA!!
TRIP..
BARF!

HAW HA
I'M SORRY, DOGGIE!
RAR-
RRAR
CRY
HA
HEE
WHEE

"NOT IN THIS FOR THE GLORY??" OH, BRU-THER!! YOU HAVEN'T THE LEAST IDEA, DO YOU!

?

HEE

HAWL

HA-HEH

YOU REALLY ARE THE GREATEST EVER, PULLAPART BOY!
YEAH, THE GREATEST!
HA HAH HAH
HEE-HE

WHITE FLOWER DAY
HEY, JOHNNY DONUTS! JAMES WATCH...
SPENCE?
?
WHAT ARE YOU DOING HERE?
YEH
SAME AS YOU, I GUESS...
You're invited
I GOT ONE OF THESE...
White Flower Day
to a Party!
WHEN: JULY 3 2000, 12 Noon
WHERE: the Old School, Room 3
RSVP: Enter 1 at a time!

WE GOT ONE, TOO!!
OH, SPENCE, YOU HAVEN'T MET THE GROCERY TWINS YET, HAVE YOU?
NUH -UH
I'M TOM
I'M DAISY
SHE'S DUMB
HE'S CRAZY
WELL, I'M SPENCE... UM, I'M SPENCE...
DUMB, AM I-
OOF!
I'LL-
YOU STARTED IT!
UGH!
?
AW, NEVER MIND THEM, SPENCE
YAH! NEVER MIND!
HMFF
HEE
BESIDES, I WANNA ASK YOU SOMETHING
ME?
21

YOU HEARD ME! WHAT'S ALL THIS "ONE AT A TIME" JAZZ? AND WHY HERE AT THE OLD SCHOOL?? IT'S SUMMERTIME, REMEMBER???

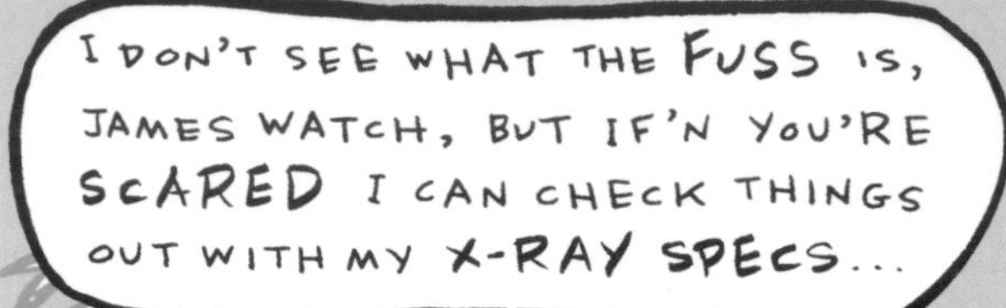
I DON'T SEE WHAT THE FUSS IS, JAMES WATCH, BUT IF'N YOU'RE SCARED I CAN CHECK THINGS OUT WITH MY X-RAY SPECS...

I THOUGHT YOU DIDN'T WEAR THOSE ANYMORE...
WELL, NOT ALL THE TIME, BUT...
LOOK'N GOOD..

I'LL EVEN GO IN FIRST...
YEP, IT'S UNLOCKED
3

CLUNK!
3

WAIT A MINUTE - THAT GUY'S X-RAY SPENCE?
YEH, OF COURSE

WHOA

IT'S O.K. - YOU CAN COME IN NOW!!

UM... HE'S WEIRD!
YEAH! THOSE GLASSES ARE HIP!!
WHERE DO YOU EVEN KNOW HIM FROM?
HE LIVES NEAR JOHNNY
AW, HE'S COOL...
I'LL SAY! I'M GOING IN NEXT!..
NO, TOM!
OH, FOR GOODNESS' SAKE, YOU GUYS! I'LL GO...
AW!..
3
4
CLUNK
NOW?
NO!!

"ONE AT A TIME", REMEMBER?
!!
ARGH

3
4
CLUNK

I DON'T SUPPOSE YOU MIND IF I GO IN NOW..?
I DON'T CARE!
21

3

2
3
4
CLUNK!

GRR!
RRRRRR!!
HELLO?
CLUNK
HEY, THIS IS ROOM THREE?
YOU GUYS?
I CAN'T SEE!
OH, THERE YOU ARE...
SOME PARTY
JOHNNY?

MAN, WHAT IS IT WITH THESE STUPID FLOWERS?

HEY! I THINK YOU CAN START THE MOVIE ALREADY, YOU KNOW?
H'YUCK YUCK!.. SNIFFF
21

WHAT ARE YOU?! DEAF!?
CRACK

EEYOW!!! JOHNNY!! YOUR CHEEKS ARE LIKE
HA HA
RUB
OH, RATS

OH, RATS!
THROB!

BOO!!

OH, JAMES WATCH! WHAT A FACE TO PULL...
TAC TAC

ARE YOU TRYING TO SPOIL MY PARTY?!
CRAC!
WHY ME

KLUNK!!!!

YOU KNOW WHAT, GUYS? THIS IS A BRAND-NEW SPECIAL OCCASION OF OUR VERY OWN...

HAPPY WHITE FLOWER DAY!

1950
THE OLD SCHOOL
FEEL BETTER?
IT'S ALL RIGHT
JULY 3, 2000

JUNE 5, 2000
BOMB BOMB
BOMB!
UH-

OUT!! IT'S OUT!

SAY... IT IS OUT!
YES!!

NAH NAH NAH! HE WENT FOR THE BALL!!!

NICE TRY, JAMES! JOHNNY DIDN'T TOUCH IT AND SO YOU'RE OUT!!
YOU KNOW IT, TOO!
Hee Hee
B'MB

YOU ONLY SAY THAT BECAUSE YOU WANT THE FOURTH SQUARE FOR YOURSELF, DAISY!!
SO TRUE, SO WHAT

YOU'RE IN, LEAKY!
YAY!
SN'D

WELL WELL
DON'T SAY IT...!

READY?

HA!!
BOMB
BOMB

YER OUT, LEAKY!
OH NO WAY!!

YOU CAN'T DO THAT ON A SERVE!!
CAN'T I?
NO!!

TCH! BE A GOOD LOSER NOW...
HA
HA!

YOU CAN'T DO THIS TO ME!!
IT'S CHEATING!
I'M TELLING!!
WHA!

YOU'RE UP, LEFTY!
I DON'T THINK SO

I JUST REMEMBERED SOMETHING: I HATE THAT LEFTY BANKS!

HA HA HA HA HA HA HA

O-K, LET'S GO!!

I DUNNO
C'MON, GUESS! YOU'LL NEVER GUESS!!
TELL US, THEN!
B'MB

HANG ON... IS IT..?
IT'S KID MEDUSA

WHAT!?

I CAUGHT HER SPYING ON Y'ALL FROM THE BUSHES! SHE LOOKED SO LONESOME...
SHUV

...I INVITED HER TO COME PLAY WITH US!
GASP!
HEY!!

LET'S KEEP THE BACKPACK ON! WE CAN'T HAVE YOU TURNING US TO STONE NOW, CAN WE?
PLEASE
SMAC!!

THAT CERTAINLY WOULDN'T BE NICE
LET US BIND HER WITH THIS JUMPING ROPE
MY, NO!

THAT WAS GOOD THINKING THERE, DAISY
THANKS!
SO WHAT ARE WE SUPPOSED TO DO WITH HER NOW?
YEAH
B'MB
SHE LOOKS PRETTY USELESS AS FAR AS FOUR-SQUARE'S CONCERNED... SO THAT'S OUT

WELL, THEN... HOW ABOUT... HUM, WAIT - IT'S COMING TO ME NOW... IT'S, IT'S...
DODGEBALL!!
BOMB!!
I'M NEXT!!
OK...
Y'KNOW, JAMES - SINCE KID MEDUSA CAN'T SEE TO DODGE - WE CAN SCARCELY CALL THIS "DODGEBALL"
GOOD POINT, JOHNNY! I GUESS IT'S MORE LIKE "KILL THE PILL"
UH!

NAH! IT'S MUCH CLOSER TO "SMEAR THE QUEER"
I THOUGHT THOSE WERE THE SAME
YEH
YOU'RE WRONG! ALL OF YOU!! THIS IS SOME BOWLING KIND OF THING...
WHEE
HUFF!
BOMBA!
YOU KNOW WHAT, GUYS? THIS IS A BRAND NEW GAME OF OUR VERY OWN...
BUB-A BUBBA
MONSTER-BALL!!

YOU KNOW... I HEARD WHERE IF YOU CUT OFF A GORGON'S HEAD, YOU'LL FIND A TINY WINGED HORSE INSIDE

I WON'T TELL...

HOLD IT!!
RIGHT THERE!
♪!!
YOU SEE, MISS MILLIE?

SCATTER, MATES!!!
!
THERE GOES MY BACKPACK!

OH! MY...
THEY WERE CHEATING!

BE QUIET, LEAKY!
BUT...

YOU POOR DEAR! THEY HAVE YOU TIED UP LIKE A RODEO CALF!!
SN'F

THERE! NOW, LET'S GET THAT BOOK-BAG OFF YOUR FACE...
NO!! YOU MUSTN'T!

BUT...BUT WHY NOT??
CRY CRY CRY

I'M KID MEDUSA!!

OH, YOU HORRID CREATURE!! YOU KNOW YOU'RE NOT ALLOWED ON SCHOOL GROUNDS!
BAW!! BAWW!!!
I KNOW! I'M SORRY!!

NOW DO YOU SEE WHY WE HAVE SUCH RULES?! NOW DO YOU SEE!?
I'M SORRY!
SOB!
OH!! OH!

IT'S FOR YOUR OWN GOOD! YOU'VE BROUGHT THIS UPON YOURSELF, YOUNG LADY! YOU'VE ASKED FOR IT!!
I SAID I WAS SORRY!!

THE END

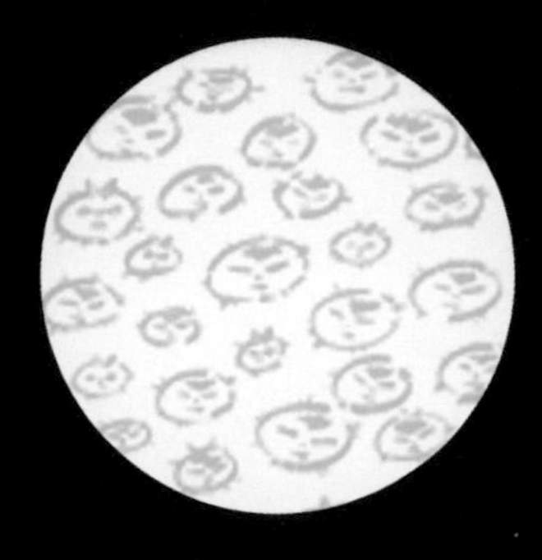

AUGUST 4,
2000

JES' CUT THE LINE, COW-BOY
I WON'T!

THIS IS MY FAVORITE OF LURES!
DIG!
FLAP FLAP
C'MON
YER GONNA KILL HIM...
DON'T WANNA
ANYWAY...

...HE BRUNG IT ON HIMSELF... SWALLOWIN' MAH HOOK SO DEEP!..
WE OUGHTTA EAT HIM!

!?
I'M NOT GONNA EAT A FISH!

WELL, WHAT'RE WE DOIN' HERE ANYHOW!
?

WE'RE JEST PASSIN' THE TIME...
HOOP!
PAP

HOW-DEE!

AW, COW-BOY
UGH

?

TCH!

HE'LL BE FINE...
DOOK!

SNIF
BAWW
WAH-WAH

HESH YER CRYIN', SIS
WAHH-BAWWW
WARSH
TAIN'T MAH TEARS...

IT'S LI'L BLOODY!
CRY
CRY

WHAT'S THE MATTER, LI'L BEE? THEY RUN YOU OFF'N THET CEMETERY, AGAIN?
NNOo
YOU KIN TELL US

WELL, YOU MAY HAVE HEARD THAT PULLAPART BOY AND I WERE TO GO CAMPING THIS WEEKEND
WE KNOW
SNUF

...YEAH, THING IS, WE WERE PACKING UP TO GO JUST THIS MORNING...
ROLL
ROLL
HH

BUT HIS FATHER, THAT PROFESSOR, HE WENT PLUMB CRAZY!
GRR!!
NO NO

HE ≥SNUF-SNUF≤ HE HAD ME BY THE SCRUFF! WHAT COULD I DO?
!!

NEXT I KNEW, HE'D GIVEN ME THE GATE!

ANYWAY, I'D SEEN PROFESSOR BOY MAD BEFORE, SO I FIGURED ON HANGING AROUND UNTIL HE SIMMERED DOWN SOME...

WELLA, HE'D COOLED OFF IN NO TIME! MARCHED RIGHT ACROSS THE STREET AND NOT TEN MINUTES HENCE HE'S BACK WITH CHUBBY AND MRS. CHEEKS IN TOW...
OH!
...BAGS AND ALL!

"SWEET" CHUBBY!
HE'S NOT SO SWEET
ARE YA SURE ABOUT ALL THIS?

I SAW THEM— SAW THEM GO!!
FLIP!
FLOP

"SWEET" CHUBBY CHEEKS...
COULD BE TROUBLE
GORSH

THEY'RE UP T'WILD HORSE VALLEY, NO?
IT'S ONLY A DAY'S RIDE
A'YUH

GOOD FISHIN' UP THET WAY...
WON'T BE A TOTAL LOSS
AH RECKON

OH, I JUST KNEW I COULD COUNT ON YOU GUYS..!

?

COW-GIRL?
COW-BOY?
YES, LI'L BLOODY

YOU GUYS KNOW WHERE WE'RE GOING, RIGHT?
YES...
...LI'L BLOODY...

EVEN IF WE FERGOT, HAZEL HORSE HERE KNOWS THE WAY BACK TO WILD HORSE VALLEY
DON'T'CHA GURL?
PAT PAT

IT'S WHERE SHE'S FROM!
OH
FSHH
D'MP
D'MP

NOW, LET ME ASK YEW SOMETHIN', LI'L BEE...
PLEASE
PULL
CHAMP

WELP, Y'ALL'VE PLANNED TH'WHOLE SUMMER T'GO CAMPING THIS WEEKEND...
UH-HUM
KICK KICK

BUT TODAY, OUT OF THE BLUE, PROFESSOR BOY GIVES YUH THE BOOT AN' TAKES THEM CHEEKS INSTEAD..?
D'MP D'MP

YES, "OUT OF THE BLUE" YOU'VE DESCRIBED IT PERFECTLY!
HUM
KLOP
O-K, BUT WHY IS IT SO?

HE JUST HATES ME, IS ALL...
AH

BUT HE MUSTA SAID SOMETHIN', LI'L BLOODY..!
HUM! OH

MY SCIENCE EXPERIMENTS!

YOU'RE THE REASON IT DOESN'T WORK GOOD!!
CLUTCH
WHA

HIS SCIENCE EXPERIMENTS!
OR SOMETHING ...YEAH...
WHAT DOES IT MEAN?
KLOP
KLOP

IT MEANS HE HATES ME!

OK-OK!! SO HE HATES YOU!
GIDDAP!
SPL'SH!
K'DNK
K'DNK!

YES, HE DOES

DOOOK

SWIM FER TH' GLUG
THE RIVERBANK!
GLAH
DON'T LOSE OUR GEAR!

WHAR'S THE SADDLE BAG! WHAR'S THET HAZEL HORSE!?
KAF KAF
LOOK'A YONDER!
YEAHHH

HO
HO
HO

AW, HAZEL!

AH RECKON SHE DIDN'T WANT T'GO BACK TA WILD HORSE VALLEY AFTER ALL...
P'TCH

WHEE
HUH-HUH!

DO YOU MEAN TO SAY HAZEL HORSE DID THAT ON PURPOSE?
SHORE
AH DO

SHE'S DONE IT BEFORE THIS
REALLY
WAIT!
WAIT WAIT!

BEFORE ANYTHING - ANYTHING! - WE MUST AGREE TO AGREE!!
AGREED!

GO!

OOH

AH!

IT'S UNANIMOUS, THEN! WE'LL CARRY ON WITHOUT HAZEL HORSE!
HURRAY!

WE'LL NEED TO DRY OUT, SO WE MAY AS WELL CAMP HERE FER THE NIGHT...
OK
LONG WALK T'MORROW

AFTER WE'VE SET UP I'LL TELL YOU HOW IT WAS HAZEL FIRST LEARN'T THET TRICK...

O-K, THIS HAPPENED WAY A'FORE WE EVER MET UP WITH HAZEL HORSE

...WHEN SHE WAS JEST A YEARLING, HAZEL WANDERED FAR FROM HER FRIENDS AND INTO THE HILLS ABOVE WILD HORSE VALLEY...

LOST IN A COLTISH REVERIE, HAZEL PAID LITTLE ATTENTION TO THESE UNFAMILIAR SURROUNDINGS.

IT'S OF LITTLE SURPRISE THEN, THAT SHE FAILED TO NOTICE URSULA, THE GRIZZLY CUB, IN THE BRANCHES HIGH ABOVE, PESTERING A LOCAL WOODPECKER.

NOW FRECKLES, LIKE MOST WOODPECKERS, WAS FAR TOO BUSY TO ENTERTAIN A YOUNG BEAR'S FOOLISHNESS.

SO, WITH ENOUGH OF HIS MORNING WASTED ALREADY, FRECKLES DISPATCHED THE IMPUDENT CUB.
POCKY

BAWW!

OF COURSE HAZEL, HAPPILY GRAZING BELOW, WAS PURTY SHOCKED TO FIND SHE NOW HAD A PASSENGER ABOARD. HER FIRST RIDER EVER!
PAUNCH!!
!?

SPOOKED, HAZEL HORSE TRIED HER BEST TO THROW THE YOUNG GRIZZLY FROM OFF HER BACK ... BUT LITTLE URSULA HELD FAST!
HEE-HE!

SOON, THE YOUNG COLT FOUND HERSELF TIRING AND, STRANGELY, GROWING USED TO THE EXTRY BAGGAGE...

WHEN HAZEL HORSE TOOK A MOMENT TO MEET HER PASSENGER, URSULA SURPRISED HER WITH A KISS, THANKING HAZEL FOR THE RIDE.

"OKEY, YOU TWO," FRECKLES SCOLDED, "RUN ALONG AND LEAVE ME TO MY WORK!"

AND SO THE NEW FRIENDS RODE TOGETHER INTO THE WOODS...

THEY HADN'T GOTTEN VERY FAR, THOUGH, WHEN HAZEL HEARD A MOST PECULIAR LOWING IN THE DISTANCE.

URSULA HEARD IT AS WELL, AND SHE BLEATED A CUBBY REPLY.

ABOVE THEM, FRECKLES LOOKED UP FROM HIS LABORS AND DECLARED "THAT YOUNG BEAR IS DETERMINED TO RUIN SOMEBODY'S DAY."

THET OLE WOODPECKER KNEW HIS STUFF! NEARBY, URSULA'S MOTHER, BIG DELLA, WAS LOOKING TO FETCH HER NAUGHTY CUB FER URSULA'S MORNING NAP.

THET NAUGHTY NAUGHTY BEAR CUB! HAZEL THOUGHT SHE WAS FUNNY, AT FIRST...

BUT WHEN THE LOWING GOT A'CLOSER, HAZEL HORSE BEGUN T'GET NERVOUS.

"HESH-UP A SECOND," SHE SCOLDED URSULA, THET NAUGHTY LITTLE GRIZZLY BEAR CUB!..

...THE NAME OF THIS STORY IS "LOOK OUT FOR BIG DELLA!"
UH-UH
HUARGHH!
CRATCH
MA!
WWAH!

BIG DELLA CHASED THEM YOUNG'UNS ALL THROUGH THOSE HILLS...

...WITH HAZEL-ALL THE WHILE-A'TRYIN' T'GIT THET CUB OFF'N HER BACK

...AND URSULA-JES' THE SAME-HOLDIN' TIGHT!
WHAA
HA HA

WELL, 'FORE TOO LONG, HAZEL HAD RUN CLEAR OUTTA FOREST AND SMACK INTO RIVERBANK...
EEK
SKIDDD

SHE WISELY FIGURED THET OLE MAMA BEAR T'BE THE FASTER SWIMMER, AND RUN ALONG THE BANK LOOKIN' FER A CHANCE'T DOUBLE-BACK.
MAH
MAH

BUT BIG DELLA WAS NOBODY'S FOOL! SHE STAYED RIGHT ON HAZEL'S TAIL, ALLUS KEEPIN' THESE YOUNG'UNS BETWIXT HER AND THE RIVER.

HAZEL HORSE WAS A'RUNNIN' OUTTA STEAM. SHE KNEW SHE COULDN'T OUTRUN THE BEAR ON THET ROCKY RIVERBANK...

THEN SHE ESPIED A DEEP HOLE IN THE WATER AND HAZEL DECIDED TO TAKE A MIGHTY GAMBLE...

...IT HAD PAID OFF! THE SHOCK OF COLD WATER HAD SHAKEN YOUNG URSULA OFFEN HER.
WHEE HEE!
BAWWW

PROBLEM WAS, BIG DELLA'D GOT SO MAD ALL SHE COULD SEE WAS HORSE HORSE HORSE!

HEEDLESS A'HER OWN KIN, SHE KEPT RIGHT ON AFTER POOR HAZEL HORSE...
DOUCHE!

AH GOTTA SAY, THINGS LOOKED PRETTY GRIM FER THE YEARLING
SWIM
SWIM
SWIM

...THOUGH MAYBE A TETCH GRIMMER FER LITTLE URSULA...

FOR, Y'SEE, THEY'D ALL RUN CLEAR UP OUTTA WILD HORSE VALLEY AND PUT IN ABOVE THE FAMOUS FALLS!

BIG DELLA, BLINDED BY HER RAGE, HADN'T RESCUED HER MISCHIEVOUS CUB WHEN SHE HAD THE CHANCE...
MEH!

NOW, OF COURSE, IT WAS TOO LATE...
MEAHHH

BOING!

SEEING HER VERY OWN DARLING BABY GO OVER THE FALLS TOOK ALL TH' FIGHT OUTTA BIG DELLA

HAZEL RAN ALL THE WAY BACK TO WILD HORSE VALLEY. A LITTLE OLDER, A LITTLE SMARTER, MAYBE

IN THE VALLEY THAT DAY WAS THIS KINDLY OLE COUPLE - FOREST RANGERS, MIND YOU - JES' TAKIN' THE AIR...
?

THEY PLUCKED THET NEAR DROWNED CUB, URSULA, OUT OF THE DRINK AND THEY RAISED HER AS THEIR OWN.
HOOO

...AND THE END IS SHE BECAME A FOREST RANGER HERSELF!

I LIKE HOW YOU ALWAYS PUT WATERFALLS IN YOUR STORIES...
G'NIGHT
Z

O-K, LI'L BLOODY
LET'S TAKE IT FROM TH' TOP!
OH, MAN!
YOU COPS ARE ALL ALIKE!!
!

IF, BY THAT YEW MEAN WE MAKE THOROUGH OUR INVESTIGATINS, YEW ARE CORRECT

I TOLD YOU GUYS! PROFESSOR BOY JUST HAS IT IN FOR ME!

THET JES' DON'T ADD UP, LI'L BEE

HE COULDA SAID ANYTHING, BUT HE BLAMED YA FER HIS SCIENCE EXPERIMENT!
THINK ABOUT IT!
THAT'S RIGHT
?

IT'S NOT AS IF HE CAN FAKE THE SCIENCE, SO YOU MUSTA DONE SOMETHING!
YEH
SEE?

LEVEL WITH US, LI'L BLOODY, WE'RE YER FRIENDS
YEAH!
OW!
PUSH
HIT

OK-OK!
MAYBE I DID MESS UP HIS OL' EXPERIMENTS!
YUH GOT ME!

ALL-RIGHT, LET'S HAVE IT
SPILL

WELL, P-BOY AND I WE'RE MESSING AROUND IN THE LAB

...AND WE, Y'KNOW, CONTAMINATED HIS, UH, SAMPLE

THAT'S IT!?
UHH
WHAT IS THAT?!

WE'VE COME ALL THIS WAY WITH YA, LI'L BLOODY, YEW GOTTA GIVE US SOMETHING!
AW!
SLAP!

BUT ... YOU GUYS KNOW I'M NO GOOD AT REMEMBERING
GRR
LOOK!
KIKH

WE'LL HELP YA THROUGH IT, STEP-BY-STEP, OKEY?
CHOC

WHAT WERE YOU DOING IN PROFESSER BOY'S LABORATORY?
I SAID! JUST MESSING AROUND
CLIC..

WHERE WAS PROFESSER BOY?
I DON'T KNOW!
CLIC!

BUT HE WEREN'T THERE, WERE HE?
NNOO

HOW'D YOU GIT INTO HIS LAB, THEN?
AH!
HAW HAW HAW
POW
POW POW!

IT-IT'S EASY FOR ME! TO GET INTO PLACES...
HERE I AM.
OPEN UP
MIST MIST

THAT'S RIGHT, AH FERGOT ABOUT IT
WHAT FOR DID YOU DO THET, ANYHOW?

PULLAPART BOY! HE WANTED TO SHOW ME HIS FATHER'S NEW EXPERIMENT
JUST LOOK AT IT!
GIMME

WHAT NEW EXPERIMENT??

SUH-SOMETHING TO DO WITH GERMS LIKE... HIS OWN GERMS, RIGHT?
WOW
THEY LOOK JUST LIKE HIM!

THE PERFESSER'S OWN GERMS?
EEECH
RUB

P-BOY WAS PRETTY HOPPED UP ABOUT IT, TOO
RIP!

HE DOESN'T GET TO WORK ON NEW EXPERIMENTS UNTIL HE FIXES THIS ONE

AHH... THEM STITCHES
WAIT A MINUTE
WHA?
SHUF

WHEN DID THIS HAPPEN??
?
HAH
G'RB

NEVER MIND IT! WHATEVER HAPPENS NEXT??
OHH
TAP
HEE

P-BOY HAD THIS IDEA HE WANTED SOMMA MY BLOOD
OH, I SAY..!
YOU'LL FIND MORE...
GO AHEAD

JAB!!
WOW!!

WHAT WAS WRONG WITH MY ARM?!

CHEEK BLOOD'S FRESHER
TAC TAC

HUM

AH THINK WE HAVE SOME QUESTIONS FER P-BOY, AS WELL...
Yup
WHEE

LET'S GO FIND HIM, THEN!
C'MON

WHAP!!

CHAMP!!

SHAKE!

TOSS

SMACK!

HYAH!
GIT!!
KAPOW
POW POW!

UGH!
AARGH
H'YA-H'YAH!!
POW POW
P-POW WOW
G'WAN!

YOWL
...AN' STAY GIT!!
POW
WOW
POW!
MANGEY BEAST!

AW, UGH
SHH

I DON'T FEEL SO GOOD...

WHUT'RE WE T'DO, COW-BOY?
DO?

YOU GOTTA BURY ME IN THE GROUND

OH, LI'L BLOODY!! DON'T SAY THAT!

...IT'S AN OLD REMEDY, COW-GIRL, DON'T WORRY

I'LL BE FINE IN A DAY OR TWO, YOU'LL SEE!
KAF

ANOTHER DAY... WASTED!
AH KNEW WE SHOULD A BRUNG A SPADE

WE'D A'LOST IT IN THE RIVER, ONLY
DURN THET HAZEL HORSE

AH'M HOLDING P-BOY RESPONSIBLE FER THIS
HESH!

AAOWW!
THUD!!

I'M IN A LOT OF PAIN HERE!!
SORRY
LI'L BEE

JUST COVER ME UP, WILL'YA?
OK OK
SNIF
KICK

WHO'S SNIFFING!
?
CRY CRY

AW, COW-GIRL!
I'M SORRY! AH CAIN'T HELP IT!!
SNUF

IT'S JEST SO SAD!!
WAH

TELL ME ANOTHER
THET WAS MAH LAST ONE...
PLEASE
AH'M TARD

AW, AH'LL TELL YA ONE, LI'L BLOODY
OH, WOULD YOU? ABOUT HAZEL HORSE?

NO NO NO! THIS'UNS ABOUT "SWEET" CHUBBY'S OLD MAN!
!?

IT'S TRUE! HIS PAW'S SERVING TIME UPSTATE FER THE ATTEMPTED **MURDER** OF A KNOWN ASSOCIATE OF HIS. I READ THE FILE LAST MONTH ON A FIELD TRIP...

THEY CALL HIM "CHOCOLATE" CHEEKS AND HE'S A **BIG**, FAT CONFIDENCE MAN. THE GUY HE TRIED TO KILL WAS HIS PARTNER ACTUALLY. "PUDGEY" PAWSON'S HIS MONIKER... HE'S UPSTATE, TOO.

BEFORE THESE TWO GRIFTERS WERE POPPED, BEFORE CHEEKS TRIED TO SUFFOCATE PAWSON, THEY USED TO RUN THE "RAG" AND "WIRE" CONS UP AND DOWN THE EASTERN SEABOARD...

"PUDGEY" PAWSON WAS THE OUTSIDE-MAN, TRAVELLING TOWN-TO-TOWN ON THE LOOK-OUT FOR SUCKERS TO FLEECE. CHEEKS ALWAYS PLAYED THE INSIDE PART OF THE CON LIKE HE WAS BORN TO IT.

ANYHOW, THEY WERE A MODESTLY SUCCESSFUL PAIR, AND DID A PURTY FAIR JOB OF STEERING CLEAR OF LOCAL LAW ENFORCEMENTS, UNTIL THE DAY THEY SET THEIR SIGHTS ON A MR. GAYLORD DUBOIS OF SNOOZEBURGH
TUNKS

RRAHR
K-POW POW!

EEK!!
MRRH
THUMP
THUMP

AARGH!
POW-POW WOW!

?

THESE STUPID LITTLE THINGS!
HYA!!
I KNOW!
POW POW
HRFF! HRF!!
GRR

WAH
WHY COUL'N'T WE HAVE REAL GUNS??
AARRGH!!
POW
POW
WOW

UGH
?
SUCK SUCK SUCK

IT'S LI'L BLOODY!
SUCK
SUCK
SUCK!

OHHH
CRUMP!

"HURRAY!"
WHEO
MM... FULL
ZZZ..

C'MON DOWN, LI'L BLOODY
HI!

LET'S GIT YEW CLEANED UP...
DIRTY
STAB
STAB

BORN YET AGAIN!
PLUSH

HALLELUJAH!!

WHAT
WHAT IS IT?

YER...
TOUCH

?
DAB

A BLEEDING NOSE!!
HERE

WHUT D'YA THINK YER
AW!

IT IS ANOTHER OLD REMEDY! TRUST ME
WELL
O-K

OMP!!

TEP

HE-
HEH

YOU SEE? I FIXED IT!
YOU SEE!

I FIXED IT!!

TOUCH

HE KISSED ME!!

HEY!
KIN YA HEAR IT, GUYS?
HEAR WHAT

THE CARS! IT'S TH'ROAD INTO WILD HORSE VALLEY CAMPGROUNDS

THAT'S THE RIVER, COW-BOY
NO, NO- WAIT

I HEAR IT, TOO!
THIS WAY
OK. OK!

WILD HORSE VALLEY
WATCH FER TRAFFIC
WOO! WOO
WOO!!

REEL IN
OOP

NOW, LI'L BEE, BEFORE WE GO ANY FURTHER...
EH!
EH EH!

WHUT'S THET?
THIS IS A PERFECT DAY SO FAR
SEE

LET'S NOT RUIN IT WITH ANY MORE POLICE CHATTER!

THAT'S FINE! ONE THING, THOUGH: WHEN WE DO HIT CAMP, WHO GETS IT FIRST?

PULL-APART-THE-BOY!!
!?
OF COURSE

THERE THEY GO NOW!!
AW, NUTS!
WHERE?

THET WAS OUR RIDE HOME!

BOOT
BOOT
BOOT

AUGUST 26, 2000

HEJ

?

LI'L BLOODY

"FAT" CHUBBY CHEEKS

WE'RE GOING TO MY MOTHER'S BAKERY FOR EGG CUSTARDS, WANNA COME?

"EGG CUSTARDS" IS HARDLY MY IDEA OF A GOOD TIME

SLIP!

WELL, IT'S MORE FUN THAN MAKING YOURSELF DIZZY ON THESE SWINGS

THAT'S WHAT YOU THINK!
YEA

WHAT'D I TELL YOU?
YEAH
AWK! THEY'LL BE OUT IN A FEW MINUTES

PULL-APART-THE-BOY

YOU TAKE IT EASY ON THEM EGG-CUSTARDS NOW...

YOU'RE LIKE T'BUST A STITCH AS IT IS...
HA!

HAH!

YOU'RE ONE OF A KIND, LI'L BLOODY...
C'MON, CHUB

WELL...
WE'LL JUST SEE ABOUT THAT!